UFO ENCOUNTERS

by RITA G. GELMAN and MARCIA SELIGSON

cover photo: Si Braun

SCHOLASTIC BOOK SERVICES

NEW YORK • TORONTO • LONDON • AUCKLAND • SYDNEY • TOKYO

For: Julie, Danny, Steve, Jan, and Mitch

abbreviations for credits:

APRO: Aerial Phenomenon Research Organization, Inc.
NASA: National Aeronautics and Space Administration
NICAP: National Investigations Committee on Aerial Phenomena

12 11 10 9 8 7 6 5 4 3 2 1   4   8 9/7 0 1 2 3/8

Printed in the U.S.A.   11

Contents

Life Out There?

Life in the Universe?

One thing we know for sure: There is life on the planet Earth. The star that we call the sun gives light and warmth and life to our planet.

Suppose you were to make a tiny dot on this page and call it the sun. Then suppose you were to keep on making dots and never stop. No time out for parties or dinners, no more school, no more sleeping — just dot-making for the rest of your life.

By the time you are eighty years old, if you have covered your house, your neighborhood, your city, and all of the United States with dots, you will still not have made as many dots as there

O soaring through southern Georgia sky in late September, '73. Chester Tatum, a newspaper publisher, took the photo. UPI are stars in just the *Milky Way* galaxy. There are billions and billions and billions of stars out there. Our sun is only one of them.

And most of these stars *could* be suns for other planets of living things—even intelligent beings.

Maybe beings like us — with arms and noses and language and clothing. Or beings that are nothing at all like us — like nothing we've ever seen — like nothing we can even imagine.

If they *are* out there — those other beings — what are they doing? What are they like? Do they think about us? Do they want to get together with us?

Maybe some of them are far more advanced than we are. Maybe some of them have figured out ways to travel through space and time. Perhaps they have already visited Earth in their spaceships. Perhaps they have even been seen by some of our Earth people.

Which brings us to UFOs: Unidentified Flying Objects.

2

What Are Those Things in the Sky?

It's moving.
It's glowing.
It's streaking across the sky.
It must be a UFO!
Probably not. The sky is full of things — and most of them are not UFOs. During the day we can see birds and planes and clouds. At night we can see stars, the flashing lights of planes, and the glowing trails of meteors. All of these sky-things can be mistaken for UFOs.

There are also things happening up there that are more complex and harder to recognize. The planet Venus, for example, sometimes looks so much brighter than anything else in the heavens that it seems to be a giant, unexplainable ball of light. And as it moves westward, Venus takes on an eerie red glow — much like many people's UFOs.

Venus fools a lot of people. Astronomers know that on certain nights, when Venus is especially bright, hundreds of people will phone the police or the Air Force and say, with a lot of excitement, that they are sure they have seen a UFO.

People-made satellites fool a lot of us, too. There are dozens of them orbiting the Earth. They can be seen without binoculars ... and they *do* look like unnatural objects in the sky. When

(left) Venus "close up" (from half a million miles), as recorded by TV cameras of Mariner 10 in flyby. A neighboring planet of Earth, Venus is often mistaken for a UFO. (right) Government weather balloons often look like UFOs.

NASA   National Center for Atmospheric Research

Lenticular clouds. Strange cloud formations like these are frequently mistaken for UFOs.

someone reports a UFO, scientists check their satellite charts.

They check the weather balloons, too. There are thousands of them up there sending down weather reports. And some of them have lights which are often mistaken for UFOs.

Strange clouds sometimes appear like mysterious flying craft. So do tornadoes. And certain kinds of lightning can seem to be fiery, fast-moving balls.

People are often confused by all those things in the sky. The scientists are not. They can easily determine that many UFOs are not UFOs at all.

When a UFO is reported, scientists, the police, the military, and ordinary citizens whose hobby it is to study UFOs come to the spot and check out the possibilities. Seventy percent of all UFO reports turn out to be natural effects or people-made objects. A few turn out to be hoaxes — stories that people make up.

But one out of five of all these reported sightings of UFOs turn out to be *real* UFOs—abnormal things in the sky that cannot be explained or identified.

There have been 70,000 or more reported sightings from all over the world. Some of them are reports of distant objects in the sky. Some of them are of craft that have landed in places very close to the witness. And some are strange tales of alien creatures who walk and talk.

Many of the stories are carefully investigated. In some cases there are pictures. In some, investigators have found holes in the ground or burnt spots on trees. Many of the cases sound absurd, many convincing.

But remember: a UFO has never landed on the south lawn of the White House. News people have never been given an interview with a being from a spacecraft. And a UFO has never crashed in the desert so that we could examine it.

We don't know whether UFOs exist. We know

that cocker spaniels and television sets exist, but not UFOs.

And, if they do exist, we really don't know what they are, where they come from, or what they're doing here. UFOs are a huge mystery.

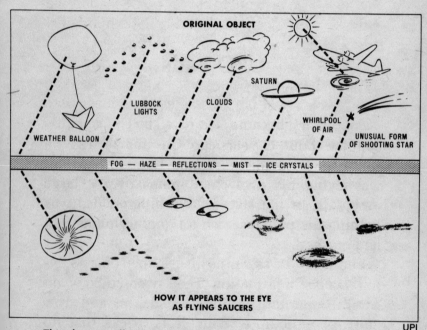

ORIGINAL OBJECT

LUBBOCK LIGHTS

CLOUDS

SATURN

WHIRLPOOL OF AIR

UNUSUAL FORM OF SHOOTING STAR

WEATHER BALLOON

FOG — HAZE — REFLECTIONS — MIST — ICE CRYSTALS

HOW IT APPEARS TO THE EYE AS FLYING SAUCERS

UPI

This drawing illustrates one astronomer's explanation for UFO sightings back in 1957.

3

UFO Fads

People first became fascinated by UFOs in this country about 30 years ago. On June 24, 1947, a salesman from Idaho, named Kenneth Arnold, was flying his own small plane over a large mountain in the state of Washington. He was helping the police search for another plane that had crashed.

Suddenly, he saw nine disc-shaped objects flying in a chain formation. They swerved between several mountain peaks, flipped over and over and did incredible flying feats, tricks that no normal airplane could do.

Arnold clocked their speed. It was over one thousand miles per hour!

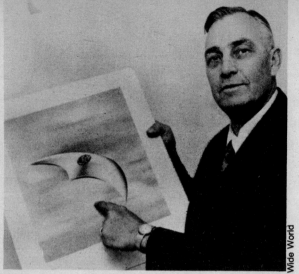

First UFO spotter! Kenneth Arnold, the Boise businessman who started the UFO fad in 1947, points to a drawing he made after a sighting near Mt. Rainier in Washington. Pulsating light came from dark spot, he said.

When the newspaper picked up his astonishing story, one reporter called the objects "flying saucers."

After Arnold's sighting of "flying saucers," hundreds and hundreds of people said that they too had seen unexplained objects in the sky.

"It looked like a stunted dill pickle," said one. "Like a hard-boiled egg cut in half," said another. "A saucer." "A hat." "A football." "A fish." "A balloon." "A pancake." "A doughnut." "A dish."

The reports piled in. The Air Force and police phones were jammed with calls from people who said we were being invaded by "flying saucers" from outer space. The government got worried. Could *all* these people be crazy? Maybe we *were* being invaded.

So the Air Force began an official study of UFO reports. And more than five million people began an unofficial hobby: collecting UFO stories. UFOs became a fad. Like skateboarding or baseball cards or T-shirts with slogans.

Fads come and go. In the last 30 years, there have been times when the conversation at supper tables all around the world was about UFOs. And other times when almost no one thought about them.

The movie *Close Encounters of the Third Kind* has been incredibly popular. Millions of families have stood in line to watch this film about UFOs and how they affected a little town in Indiana. In classrooms, on street corners, at parties, UFOs are again a big topic.

Melinda Dillon, as Jillian Giuler, and Cary Guffey, as her son Barry, watch something extraordinary taking place outside their home in *Close Encounters of the Third Kind*.

4

What Do They Look Like?
What Do They Do?

One of the most interesting things about UFOs is that they have a lot in common. No one has ever reported a UFO that looked like a palm tree. And there are no reports of UFOs that are shaped like horses. Or elephants. Or vacuum cleaners.

Nearly all UFO sightings fit into certain patterns:

• *UFOs are usually seen in places where there are very few people, almost never around big cities. And, usually, they are seen between midnight and 8 A.M.*

Farmers often see UFOs. Policemen patrolling

lonely roads. Hunters. Fishermen. People out for walks in the woods.

Is this because lonely people tend to see imaginary things? Or perhaps it's because the UFOs are afraid of crowded, well-lighted cities.

• *UFOs often happen in "flaps": hundreds of reports in one year, usually in one or two special areas. And then very few for several years. And then another "flap."*

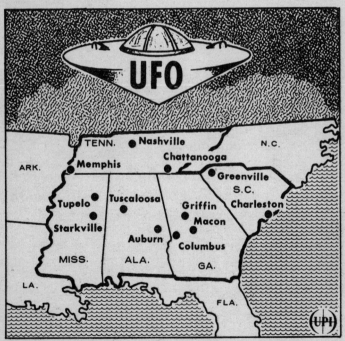

UFO fad, 1973. Spots on map indicate areas where mysterious flashing lights were reported by hundreds of Southerners in early October, 1973.

Is it because people like to be a part of the group, and when a few reports become famous, lots of people are encouraged to join the excitement? Or perhaps it's because somewhere out there in space one little guy says to his friends, "Hey, let's check out Chicago this year." And they hop into their flying machines and take off.

• *The shapes of UFOs usually fall into the following categories: tops, jellyfish, saucers, hats, circles (usually seen at night as fiery balls), and cigars.*

• *UFOs can supposedly fly in ways that our science has not yet developed. They can go straight up and down, make right-angle turns, stop and start at incredible speeds, and zig-zag through the air. They can appear or vanish at will, or many can merge into one.*

• *The most common noises that come from UFOs are reported to be buzzing, whistling, absolute silence, and, sometimes, explosions.*

In April of 1957, in a tiny village in France, a remarkable UFO sighting was made. Two local women were walking on a road one afternoon when they were startled by a monstrous noise. Turning around, they saw a strange object flying slowly, just a few feet above the ground. It was shaped like a big top, with many metallic antennae on the upper part. The antennae shook back and forth fiercely, and as they did, the road signs began shaking too. The UFO landed. The women shrieked.

A short distance away, a farmer was working in his field when he heard a deafening noise. He thought it was an auto crash. Then he saw the craft leaping through the air. He, too, saw road signs vibrating loudly as the UFO passed over them.

UFO sighted in Rouen, France, in March, 1954. Considered by *RAF Flying Review* to be one of the few photos which seem authentic.   NICAP

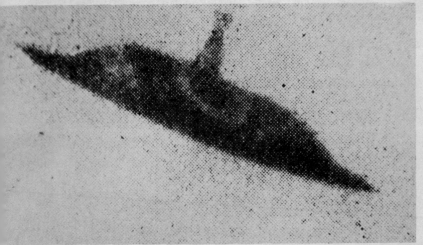

This case was investigated thoroughly by the French police, scientists, and the French "FBI." The witnesses were thought to be trustworthy. The same UFO was even spotted by two other people in a neighboring village, so this story was taken seriously.

• At night, most UFOs send out a fiery glow or lights that change color and intensity.

A captain in the U.S. Air Force, Larry Coyne, was flying a helicopter one night in Ohio. Three crew members were with him. Suddenly they saw a weird red light on the horizon. It was coming toward them at enormous speed—on a direct collision course. If both vehicles continued in the same way, they would crash. Coyne was forced to put the chopper into a steep dive.

When the red light was within 500 feet, the crew saw what it was: a metallic-gray, cigar-shaped UFO, with a dome on top and a red light in front.

The two vehicles were about to collide at 1500 feet elevation when the UFO suddenly changed speed and direction. It hovered close to the helicopter as if investigating it. It beamed a dazzling green light into the cockpit. Then, it turned and sped away.

Captain Coyne noticed that his controls were still set for the dive, but his elevation was now 3800 feet. The helicopter had soared 2300 feet up without the controls being changed and with no sensation of lifting!

Pilots have seen more UFOs than anybody else. It is easy to understand why — they spend more time in the skies than anybody else. Also, they are reliable witnesses, since they're used to seeing natural things like meteors and person-made things like weather balloons. They also see UFOs at closer range than land-bound people. So a lot of stories of sightings come from airplane pilots and stewardesses.

First thought to be a UFO, this photo was taken by astronaut James McDivitt on the Gemini 4 spaceflight in 1965. Later, McDivitt explained that the sun's rays struck a metal bolt, causing a flare in the camera lens. NASA

• Many people who have met UFOs say that their car engines stopped, their headlights went out, their radios just went dead.

It was 8:30 one morning in March, 1963, when a businessman was driving to work. Suddenly, his car stalled and it wouldn't start again.

The man looked out the window. He saw something in the field nearby that seemed like a giant top. The thing had an orange glow around it and it was hanging suspended in the air.

A few minutes later, the object disappeared. At that moment, the man noticed that there was a car behind him. He spoke to the driver. The other car had stalled also. And the other driver had seen the object. Both cars then drove off without any engine problems.

• Animals are often upset by the presence of UFOs.

Many of the people who report sighting UFOs say that their animals were the first to notice something strange. "My dogs started howling." "The horses were kicking." "The bull was banging his pen."

• *One of the strangest reports about some UFOs is that they send out beams of light or energy that can cause skin rashes and light burns, and can heal wounds.*

In southern France, in 1968, there was a well-known and respected doctor. We have to call him "Doctor X," because he doesn't want his real identity to be revealed. Dr. X wants no publicity. He has never told his story to his patients. He has never even told it to his friends. His story is *that* peculiar.

On the rainy night of November 1st, the doctor and his family were asleep in their house. At about 4 A.M., he was wakened by the cries of his 14-month-old son. The baby was motioning excitedly toward the window from his crib. Right outside, through the rain, the doctor saw flashes of brilliant light, which he assumed to be lightning.

He walked through the house checking the windows for leaks, calmly preparing a drink of water for the baby. The lights continued flashing rapidly, but they came only from one side of the house.

Then the doctor opened a large window leading onto a terrace and saw them — two disc-shaped objects, silvery white on top and red underneath. Each one had an antenna sticking out on top.

Flashes of light shot out from the discs about every second. As the doctor watched, the discs moved closer and closer to the house. Then an astonishing thing happened: the antennae from both discs connected with each other; the flashing stopped; and the two UFOs actually joined into one!

Now there was only one craft. It kept moving nearer to the doctor. When the craft was very close, a beam of light from the disc shone directly into the doctor's face and covered his entire body in light. Suddenly a loud "BANG" was heard and the disc simply vanished.

The most peculiar part of this whole UFO story is what happened to the doctor afterward, long after the disc had disappeared. Three days earlier he had hurt his leg chopping wood and still had a big swelling and painful bruise. He was walking with a bad limp. Right after his encounter with the UFO, he woke his wife to tell her what had happened. And then she noticed that the bruise and swelling, and even the limp, were completely gone. The pain was gone too.

A few days after that the doctor realized that another wound—an old one from the war that he had carried for years — had also healed.

Then, a red triangle appeared on his stomach for no reason. The next day the same marking was right there on his baby's belly too.

For several years afterward, there was no recurrence of the old war wound. But the odd triangle would appear from time to time. It would come to the father and son *at the same time,* even when they were separated by a great distance.

Doctor X has kept this amazing adventure a secret for all of these years.

UFOs. Are they or aren't they? One of the most convincing arguments for their existence is the fact that there are so many similar stories. They

UFO photographed by a Peruvian architect outside Lima in October, 1973

UPI

come from all parts of the world — from South American businessmen, French children, American pilots. From astronomers, clergymen, farmers. So many people have told similar stories that scientists have been forced to consider the stories seriously.

UFO snapped from a research ship near Trinidade Isle, Brazil, in January, 1958. The photo is considered authentic by government sources.

5

Getting In on the Action

Spotting a UFO can be fun and exciting. People get their pictures in the paper. Reporters and investigators interview them. Friends and neighbors ask a lot of questions, pay a lot of attention. And maybe, if the UFO is particularly interesting or different, the one who spotted it is invited to be on television talk shows or to lecture to groups around the country. There's a buzz of activity around the person who spots a UFO...and it's terrific to be in on the action. There can be money as well.

Maybe it was the money that was in the heads of two men that we'll call George and Henry. They were harbor patrolmen, they said, and they were out in their patrol boat on June 31, 1947, with a crew, a boy, and a dog.

They were patrolling near Maury Island in Puget Sound, when everyone noticed six objects in the sky. The objects were shaped like doughnuts and they were headed toward the boat. They were silver and silent, with portholes all around the edges.

When the objects were about 500 feet over-head, they stopped. One of them seemed to be in trouble. The others circled around the disabled craft. Then one of the "healthy" craft touched the one in the middle. The two remained in contact for a few minutes.

Suddenly there was a bang, and pieces of metal fell from the sky. Then, a different and harder material fell. The boat was damaged. The boy was hurt. The dog was killed.

The men scooped up some of the metal from the beach and rode back to the mainland. They tried to call for help, but there was too much interference on the radio.

The men sent some of the metal to a magazine, along with their story. The publisher sent some-one out to investigate.

It turned out that the whole story, from beginning to end, was a hoax! There were no "doughnuts," no pieces of metal falling from the sky. There wasn't even a boy or a dog.

In fact, George and Henry weren't even patrolmen. They were just a couple of guys with beat-up boats and very active imaginations.

Many reports of UFOs turn out to be like that one — hoaxes.

November 9, 1974, was a dark Saturday night in Carbondale, Pennsylvania. There wasn't much to do, so the three teenage boys went out by the pond. Suddenly, they later reported, a whirling, beaming object floated down from the sky and splashed into the water. The boys called the police to report a UFO.

A crowd gathered as the police arrived. The object was still glowing from the bottom of the pond. The police shot at it. But the light still shone eerily through the dark water.

Soon someone came over to the pond and announced that he was from the Center for UFO Studies in Illinois. He told the local crowd that it was dangerous to send scuba divers into the water to get the object. If it turned out to be radioactive, he said, the water would be contaminated.

So plans were made to drain the pond. But before doing so, the local police chief decided to let one scuba diver go down. It seemed safe, as there had been no signs of radioactivity.

The diver put on his equipment as the excited crowd argued about his safety. He plunged into the water and swam along the murky bottom until his hand touched the glowing object. When he came to the surface, the diver held the object up so everyone could see.

It was a waterproof flashlight.

Just in case there weren't enough UFO hoaxes to plague the scientists and investigators, the following ad appeared in the Philadelphia *Inquirer* on November 12, 1974:

"FOR SALE: SIMULATED SAUCER. Be the first in your block to create a real scare. Breaks down quickly and packs in ordinary station wagon for fast getaway. Glows in many colors and provides simulated radiation effect. Saucer creates radio and TV interference in one-mile radius. Will not fly and is not to be confused with CIA models. Set up saucer beside a road and watch for fast results! Then be the first on the scene to 'investigate' the sighting and get fat interviews with newspapers and bigtime UFO researchers.''

Is this a UFO? This flaming object was photographed by a Utica, NY, boy from his backyard in April, 1966, and seen by thousands of others.

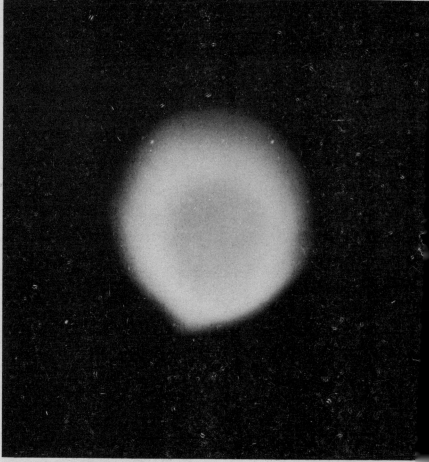

Barium cloud formed after NASA launching of experimental rocket from Virginia in September, 1966. The huge multi-colored cloud resulted in many reported sightings.

The rash of UFO sightings in southwestern U.S. in 1966 and 1967 was linked by some to a government space project called Voyager. A Columbus (OH) Dispatch reporter photographed this space vehicle at White Sands, NM.

Quick, Somebody, a Camera!

See a UFO and become an instant celebrity. Snap a picture of one and make big money. It's tempting to a lot of people.

Why not cover a frisbee with aluminum foil and toss it out for a photo? Heave a hubcap into the air and photograph "a ship from outer space."

Phony photos are easy to take, so UFO investigators must study every picture carefully. Some photos are simple to figure out; they look like what they are — hamburgers, hats, pie plates, or ping pong balls.

But many snapshots are more difficult to analyze. The investigators may have to go to the place where the picture was taken to measure distances, examine the camera, talk with the photographer, see if there were any other witnesses. Experts can study shadows in a picture and tell the height and true size of the object.

One picture studied was taken by a U.S. Coast Guard photographer on July 16, 1952. The photographer was sitting inside a building at the Coast Guard station in Salem, Massachusetts. He looked out the window and saw strange lights in the sky. He quickly snapped a photo. The lights disappeared almost immediately.

When the picture was sent to the Air Force to be studied, they decided that the "lights in the sky" were not in the sky after all; they were inside lights reflected in the window. One of the clues that led to this decision was the fact that if the lights had been in the sky, they would have been reflected in the cars. The photographer had made an honest mistake.

A picture can fool even the experts, and sometimes has. Of all the photos that have been labeled as genuine UFOs by the authorities, many many more have been pooh-poohed or put in the "we're-not-sure" category. The Rex Heflin photographs have confused even the best UFO investigators.

Rex Heflin, a traffic investigator in California, spent most of his time on the highways, driving a truck, checking on road conditions. He had a two-way radio in the truck so that he could call in to his office from time to time. He also kept a camera in his truck, the kind that takes instant photographs.

On the morning of August 3, 1965, Heflin was driving near the city of Santa Ana when he saw an object flying toward him. It looked like a giant hat or a huge plate with a bowl on top of it.

Heflin stopped and grabbed his camera. He took one picture from inside the truck and had to wait impatiently for it to develop before he could take another. Three pictures were all he could get of the craft before it sped away. His fourth photo was of a dark cloud left by the mysterious object.

While the craft was hovering near the truck, Heflin had tried to use his two-way radio; it was dead. When he returned to his office, he took the radio to the service shop. There was nothing wrong with it; it worked perfectly. One of the men in the office confirmed Heflin's story — he, too, had been listening to the radio and had heard it go dead.

Heflin's pictures were printed in the local papers. They were passed around to friends and

UPI

Rex Heflin snapped this picture of a flying object from his truck while driving near Santa Ana, CA, in August, 1965.

family and neighbors. By the time serious investigators got around to studying the case, the original photos were lost. (In order to make a serious study of a photograph to determine whether or not it is really a UFO, the original picture should be used.)

The Air Force called the whole thing a hoax. They said their studies showed that the object couldn't have been bigger than three feet, and that it was no more than 20 feet above the ground. Heflin had said that the craft was about 30 feet in diameter, eight feet thick, and 150 feet off the ground.

Rex Heflin insisted that the story was true. Was he lying? His supervisors in the traffic department vouched for the fact that Heflin was a trustworthy man: he was a valuable worker, friendly, good-natured, alert, mature, and normal in every way.

Other groups made thorough investigations of the Heflin case. They revisited the site. They studied the shadows, the truck, the camera. One group of investigators claimed the Air Force was mistaken — that if the object had been small and near the ground, there would have been a shadow on the road. There was no shadow.

Did Heflin see a UFO or didn't he? It's hard to know what to think.

7

Could They All Be Imagining It?

Some of the most intriguing stories—and most convincing—are the ones that are told by several unconnected witnesses...not a family group, not good friends, not even witnesses in the same place at the same time. Frequently people who don't know each other.

One night in 1957, a Texas policeman was sitting at his desk when a call came in. A frightened man said that a glowing, torpedo-shaped flame had just flown toward his truck. When it was just a few feet away, the truck engine stopped and the lights went out. After the flame disappeared, the engine started and the lights went back on. There was a passenger in the truck who saw exactly the same thing.

The police officer listened politely and decided that the man was probably "seeing things." Then the phone rang again.

Mr. W. related that he had been driving near the location of the first report. He saw a huge, egg-shaped, beaming object on the road. His lights went out, his engine died. The beam lit up the entire area. When Mr. W. got out of his car, the object rose and disappeared. As soon as it did, his car engine started up.

Then came the third call — bright object, engine stalled. Altogether there were 15 calls that night.

A natural occurrence? Perhaps. Maybe it was stars, meteors, or something called "ball lightning." But there was no thorough investigation and no adequate scientific explanation. Fifteen people are still wondering what they saw.

A similar series of sightings was described at Exeter, New Hampshire, in 1965. A young man watched as a brilliantly-lit object, surrounded by a circle of light, came toward him. It moved in silence, wobbling slowly through the air. Then it moved away. The man ran to the police station and returned to the scene with a policeman.

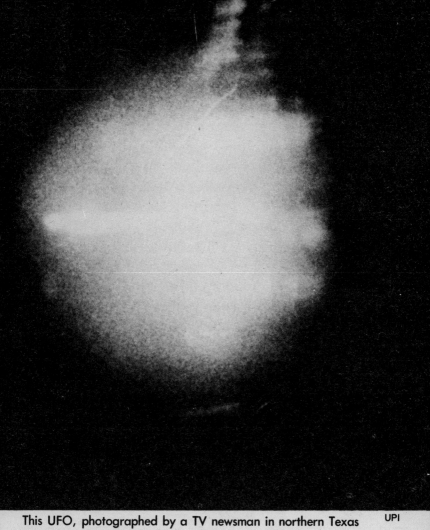

This UFO, photographed by a TV newsman in northern Texas around 3:00 A.M. in August, 1965, was similar to the one reported in Exeter, NH, that same year.

There it was again, rocking, wobbling, moving like nothing they had ever seen before. It was big, bigger than a house! The only noise around was the howling of dogs, the nervous kicking of horses.

Another policeman arrived. He, too, saw the object, slowly swaying out of sight.

A few minutes later a call came into the station. An excited telephone operator reported that she had just gotten a call from a terrified man. A "flying saucer" was after him, he screamed.

Authorities from the Pentagon made the following judgment: "We believe what the people saw that night were stars and planets in unusual formations."

That explanation may have satisfied the Pentagon, but it didn't satisfy many scientists. "Unusual formations" is not a scientific explanation.

And it certainly didn't satisfy the people of Exeter who saw the strange object. They'll never forget that night.

8

Something Was There

Somehow, it's not too hard to believe that there might be strange flying objects in our skies. That's okay. They're far up there. We're way down here. As long as they don't bother us, we won't bother them.

It gets a little harder to believe the folks who relate that they have seen those objects down here — in fields, on roads, in somebody's backyard. There they are, those weird machines, just sitting there, on our soil ... on our Earth ... doing odd tricks like whistling and glowing red and wagging their antennae.

It would be simple to claim the witnesses were mistaken about seeing a UFO. But, in some cases, there is actual evidence that something was there: holes in the ground, circles of pressed-down or burned grass, burns on the trees, marks or burns on a person's body, traces of radio-activity in the air.

One fascinating case occurred in France several years ago. A farmer happened to look out his window one evening. He saw a huge saucer-like object sitting in his field. It had a blue glow around it, and as the farmer watched in astonishment, the object moved straight upward into the heavens and vanished.

The next day the farmer went down to the field, which had been recently plowed. A huge circle of earth had been pressed down so hard, by *something*, that it was almost solid rock. All around that spot the soil was soft and ready for planting.

Over the next few years, the farmer plowed and plowed the place where the circle—and the UFO—had appeared. At first he couldn't get anything to grow in that circle. Gradually, and after much effort, living things started to grow. But, even years later, the crops in the circle would only grow to half the size of everything around it.

This case was studied by the police, the French FBI, and several scientific groups. No one felt there was any trickery.

Alien Beings

And now we come to the tough part. Other creatures. They're called "alien beings," "little people," "humanoids."

These beings are almost always described by the witnesses in the same way: about four feet tall, gray or tan in color, without hair and fingernails, and with pumpkin-shaped heads. Sometimes they are described as having no ears, or no noses, or a wide slit for a mouth; sometimes they actually speak, sometimes they "talk" through thoughts with no words; sometimes they supposedly wear helmets, brown suits, or tin foil wrapped around their bodies. Almost always, aliens are reported to be friendly, curious, and playful.

Compared to alien beings, glowing orange objects in our backyards are nothing!

Most of us have to stifle a giggle when we read stories about little people who look like they're wrapped in aluminum foil or cellophane. Little people who float and speak in strange sounds.

But let's go back for a minute. If we accept the fact that there is probably life on other planets in the Milky Way...and if we accept the fact that such life might be more advanced scientifically than we are, and that it may have discovered how to travel to Earth...and land on our ground... then why shouldn't the little beings get out of their vehicles once they're here?

But it isn't easy for anyone to accept the reports of encounters with alien beings. We have no photographs of any, although once in a while someone will play a joke. (One man bought a monkey in a pet shop, shaved its head, and painted it green. He took a picture and told people he had seen a little green man.)

Actually, there is no "hard" evidence of any sort. No alien being has ever left a footprint or forgotten its purse. The only evidence we have are the statements of witnesses. And there are many more statements than there are reliable witnesses.

There are people who like to make up stories—ghost stories, for instance, or adventure tales that never really happened. They do it because it makes them seem exciting or because it entertains their friends. That's the way it often is with UFO stories about contact with "humanoids." Some people invent these weird stories because they really think they see them. They're not lying, they're just mistaken about what they have seen.

But once we've eliminated the unreliable witnesses, we are still left with a large number of respected, responsible people who claim to have seen or talked with "alien beings." Such incidents have become known as "UFO encounters of the third kind."

● ●

The stories that follow have all been investigated seriously. The witnesses are considered to be trustworthy. Almost all of them have been given lie-detector tests to see if they are telling the truth and psychological tests to see if they are mentally healthy.

Some of them have been hypnotized. Hypnosis

is a way of helping someone remember details that she or he may have forgotten.

The stories may be hard to believe. No one is asking you to believe them. Certainly they are interesting to read and intriguing to think about and fun to talk about.

Are they true? *That* you must decide for yourself.

This UFO photo, snapped in midwest U.S. in 1967, is considered one of the most authentic ever taken.

Wide World

10

Encounters with Alien Beings

#1: The Case Of Lonnie Zamora

Lonnie Zamora, a police officer in New Mexico, was following a black Chevrolet down the highway. It seemed to be speeding. A loud roar and a distant flame distracted him from the chase.

Zamora dropped the speeding car and followed the flame off the highway and into the hills. He thought the flame might have come from an old shack that was filled with dynamite.

After a few minutes, Zamora saw a silvery object which looked like an overturned car. There were two small creatures in white overalls standing nearby. They were about the distance of two football fields away from Zamora.

When he arrived on the spot, he heard another

roar and saw another flame. This time the flame was under the object. Slowly the object rose straight up and disappeared with a great noise. Zamora called for help, and policemen arrived. Together, the men examined the area. There were deep marks in the ground where the object had rested. Some nearby plants were burned.

Investigators determined that Zamora had not lied. Something had really landed on that spot. A lunar module on a secret practice mission? Perhaps. But no record of such a mission exists.

Called by its scientist-photographer "unexplained phenomena," this UFO was sighted near Santiago, Chile, in March, 1968. It appeared at an altitude of about 6,600 feet.

#2: The Case In New Zealand

Some cases may be real, but they are impossible to prove; we just have to listen to them with an open mind. A farm woman in New Zealand was on her way to milk the cows early one morning when she saw two green lights through the clouds and found herself and the field bathed in green light. She was frightened and dove for the trees. A saucer-shaped glow descended, hovering at roof height. It was about 30 feet long and had two rows of jets that shot out orange flames.

Then the flames stopped. Inside the UFO, a light was turned on. Two "men" were inside, wearing aluminum foil suits that hugged their bodies. Their heads were covered by helmets. She couldn't see their faces.

After a few moments, the jets started flaming again and the ship shot straight up at great speed and vanished into the clouds.

The police, an Air Force representative, and an aircraft engineer all visited the woman. But nothing could be proved beyond her story.

#3: The Case of the French Children

The twelve-year-old boy, Raymond Romand, just wanted to go out for a walk. He had often taken quiet after-dinner strolls outside the family farmhouse in the little French village of Premanon. He certainly never expected to have an adventure.

Soon after he walked out, he discovered what looked like a big metal box, about the size of a door. The "box" walked over to Raymond and touched him. It was very cold.

Raymond fell to the ground, terrified. He opened his mouth to call for help, but no sounds came out. When he got back on his feet, he started to run back inside, but he changed his mind. His parents would say he was crazy. They would say he was lying.

Then Raymond's sisters came out — nine-year-old Janine and two younger girls. Janine saw the "box" and ran into the barn.

Raymond began throwing stones at the "box." It walked away. Raymond and the other children watched. The object walked to a pasture down the hill and entered a glowing red craft. The craft, which looked like a ball of fire, took off into the sky.

The children decided to keep the whole story a secret. They were afraid that their mother would punish them for lying. But the next day, Raymond told one of his classmates. The boy then told the teacher. And the teacher told the police.

Police investigators came to Raymond's house. They asked Raymond and the other children to show them the place where the craft had been resting. The police examined the area. They found a 12-foot circle of hard-packed soil and flattened grass. They found four holes in the ground. And they discovered that the bark of a nearby pine tree had been burned.

The police captain talked to the children separately. He asked them to tell him exactly what had happened. He made them go to the same places and do exactly what they had done. They all repeated exactly the same tale.

The children's mother insisted that the story was a lie. The children were punished. They weren't allowed to leave the house. And she didn't want them to talk to any more police or reporters. But neither Raymond nor his sisters ever changed their story.

Half of the people in the town of Premanon felt that the children had had a unique experience. The other half thought that they deserved a good spanking.

#4: The Case in Pascagoula

The night of October 11, 1963, wasn't much different from a lot of other quiet nights in Pascagoula, Mississippi. By 9 o'clock, some of the people in town had already gone to sleep. Most of the others were watching TV. A gas-station owner got up after watching *Kung-Fu* to get a glass of milk. He happened to look out the window. He saw a row of lights moving over the street. They were too high to be a car, he thought. They were traveling too slowly to be an airplane. He watched for awhile and then went back to the TV.

Not very far away, Charles Hickson, 42, and Calvin Parker, 18, were fishing on an abandoned

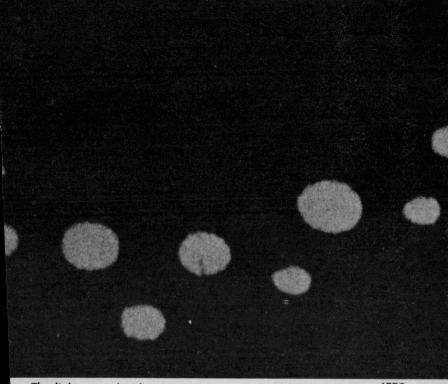

The lights seen by the gas-station owner in Pascagoula, MS, were similar to the famous Lubbock Lights (above). Photographed by Carl Hart, Jr. in August, 1951, there were many witnesses on several nights to these lights flying in formation at high altitudes over Texas.

APRO

55

pier. Charles was about to bait his hook when both men noticed a blue light in the sky.

At first, they didn't think much of it. But soon, the light came down about 35 yards away from them. It hovered about two feet off the ground. There were no blasts or explosions. No engine noises or unearthly sounds. Just a soft buzzing.

The men were terrified. Hickson said later that his arms felt as though they were frozen solid.

As the two men tried to back away from the craft one end of the vehicle opened up and three creatures came out. They had silvery wrinkled skin, claw-like hands, and a single stump instead of two legs. They were about five feet tall. They had big, bulging eyes and pointed ears and something that came straight out where a nose should be. "They didn't walk," said Hickson later. "Not the way we do. They floated."

The creatures floated around the men and lifted them up. Hickson felt no pain, no pressure. Suddenly, he was floating toward the craft with the creatures. There is some question in Parker's mind about whether or not he also floated to the craft. He thinks he passed out. Hickson, also, cannot remember.

Once inside the craft, a machine that seemed to

Hickson like a big eye moved all around him, never touching him but scanning his whole body like an X-ray machine. Hickson looked around. There were no chairs, nothing at all to sit on. Everyone was just floating about.

About 20 minutes later, the men were back on the pier. There was a buzzing sound and the craft and its creatures disappeared.

The men were unharmed but scared. Whom could they tell? Who would believe them? Everyone would think they were crazy.

At first, Hickson told Parker that they should keep the whole adventure a secret. He was afraid they would sound like fools. But later, Hickson decided that the right thing to do was to tell the story to the sheriff.

The sheriff tape-recorded their story. Both men took lie-detector tests. According to the sheriff, they passed the exams. They were telling the truth, said the machine.

Charles Hickson and Calvin Parker became instant celebrities. Newspapers across the country ran their story on page one. The men appeared on television to tell about their experience. They received thousands of letters, mostly from people who believed their story, people who were sure that Hickson and Parker were telling the truth — people who'd had UFO experiences of their own.

But even more people were sure that Hickson and Parker were lying...and a lot of people in the middle just didn't know what to think.

#5: The Case of Patrolman Schirmer

The dogs in Ashland, Nebraska, were howling more than usual on the night of December 3, 1967. A bull at the edge of town was crashing at its gate. As Patrolman Herbert Schirmer cruised along Highway 63, he wondered about the noise. It was usually quiet in Ashland at 2:30 A.M.

Just before he reached Highway 6, Schirmer noticed what he thought was a truck flashing its red lights. Schirmer turned on his high beams so that he could see more clearly. The flashing red lights disappeared into the sky.

At 3 A.M., Schirmer arrived at the police station. He wrote in the record book:

"Saw a flying saucer at the junction of Highways 6 and 63. Believe it or not."

That night Schirmer couldn't sleep. He had a buzzing in his head and a fierce headache. Then he noticed a red sore below his left ear. He had no memory of having hurt himself.

Schirmer's flying saucer was reported to a UFO investigating committee. Schirmer was hypnotized to determine if he was telling the truth.

Under hypnosis, Schirmer realized that he had no memory at all of the minutes that followed his sighting of the "truck." He could not recall *anything* that had happened between 2:30 and 2:50.

For months after he made his "missing time" discovery, Schirmer was bothered. What had happened in those 20 minutes? Why couldn't he remember?

Schirmer was getting headaches all the time now. He couldn't concentrate on his job. "You can't be a good policeman if you have personal problems," he said. And he quit.

Schirmer wanted to try hypnosis again, to get at whatever was hidden deep in his mind. He was sure that something had happened during those 20 lost minutes, and he wanted to know what it was.

So Schirmer was hypnotized again. The hypnotist told him, "You are back on Route 63. It is

2:30 in the morning on December 3, 1967...."
And then Schirmer remembered!

The "truck" had not disappeared. Schirmer had been able to follow it into a field. When he got close, he saw that it looked like a huge, silvery, glowing football. Schirmer watched as the craft set down three legs and landed on the ground. The craft was making a "whooshing" sound and flashing its lights.

Schirmer had tried to call the station, but his radio was dead. So were his lights ... and his engine. He looked out the window of his patrol car and saw strange-looking beings coming toward him.

Like patrolman Schirmer, a patrolman in Michigan also sighted a UFO. Later, with five other people, he put together this composite drawing of what they saw in southern Michigan in March, 1966.

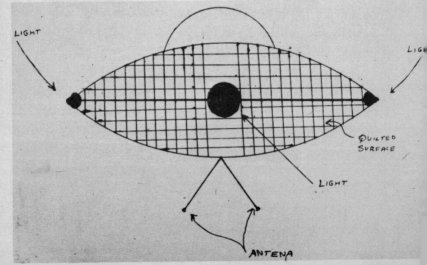

They were small and wore silver uniforms with a picture of a winged serpent on the left front side. They wore boots and gloves and helmets, close-fitting and of the same silvery substance as the uniforms. Each being wore a round walkie-talkie contraption that had an antenna. The little machine was attached where we have our left ear.

Schirmer was terrified. He tried to draw his gun. He couldn't do it. He wanted to leave. But he couldn't do that either. "Something" was making him stay. But he wasn't able to explain what that "something" was.

When the beings were next to the car, Schirmer noticed a puff of greenish gas. He felt something pressing against his neck, just below his left ear. And he saw a bright flash of light.

Then he was entering the craft. It was cold, filled with computer-like machines with buttons and tapes. The beings talked to him through their antennae. He could hear their voices but they never moved their mouths.

They told him they were from a nearby galaxy. They told him they were a small ship and they showed him, on a big screen, a view of their mother ship out in space. They told him that they have bases here on Earth, underground and underwater.

They were kind and friendly to him. They spoke to him in English, in strange-sounding, mechanical voices. Schirmer thought perhaps they were connected to computers that could speak any language.

He also had the feeling that they were able to feed ideas directly into his mind. He knew so much more about them than they had said. And his mind felt full, tired. Perhaps the red sore near his ear was a clue. Perhaps he was somehow connected to a computer!

Finally, the alien beings told him not to talk about his visit inside the ship. They told him to say only that he had seen a ship and that it disappeared. Then they took him back to his police car. Schirmer watched as the humming craft disappeared into the sky.

Schirmer's story is fantastic. It is the most detailed report of an encounter with alien beings that exists. Yet, until that night in December, Schirmer didn't even believe in UFOs. In fact, he hadn't ever thought about them. His father had been in the Air Force, so when Schirmer thought about flying things, he thought only about planes.

In December, before Schirmer quit his job and then found out what had happened to him in those lost 20 minutes, he was promoted to head of his police department. He had always been respected by the people in Ashland. Certainly if he had seen a traffic accident, he would have been considered a reliable witness. Does his astonishing story make him less reliable?

Once again, we are baffled.

#6: The Case of Travis Walton

The following case took place in a national forest in Arizona in 1975. Seven professional foresters were returning home from work in a pick-up truck. At a clearing in the woods they spotted a windowless disc, about 10 feet high and 15 feet across. It was hovering over the spot. Instantly, one of the foresters, a man named Travis Walton, leaped from the truck and ran toward the UFO. His friends tried to call him back but he wouldn't stop. When he was underneath the disc, a ray of blue light shot down on him, and either he was knocked unconscious or he vanished. The witnesses weren't sure.

His friends were frightened and drove away. But within a half-hour, they calmed down and returned to the clearing. The UFO and Travis Walton were gone. The police were called and they scoured the area for any traces. They could find nothing. The six men were given lie-detector tests and the police decided that they were telling the truth about this weird incident.

Five days after Travis's disappearance, at midnight, his brother received a phone call. It was from a phone booth several miles away. The caller was Travis, begging to be picked up. When his family reached the phone booth, which was by the side of the highway, they saw Travis—weak, unshaven, and bewildered. He didn't know what day it was and believed he had been gone only a few hours, instead of five days.

Doctors gave him a complete physical exam and found the only thing wrong with him was simple exhaustion. They were sure he was well-nourished and could not possibly have been wandering in the wilderness for those five days.

Travis remembered only the following details: Soon after he left the truck to run toward the disc, he woke up on a white examination table inside the craft. Standing over him, smiling, were three humanoids—one was a female. They were about five feet tall, with huge eyes, no hair, and no fingernails. They did not speak to him, but they examined his body thoroughly, like very curious and interested doctors. They did not harm him at all.

They left him alone on the craft for a few minutes and he wandered into another room and started pressing buttons that were on the arm of a big chair. One button opened a panel over his head through which he could see stars. A few minutes later, one of the creatures returned and led Travis to a big lighted space where several smaller UFOs were lined up. Then some other humanoids, these with hair, placed a mask over his face. Travis Walton remembered nothing else until he awoke. He was lying in the middle of a highway in Arizona.

The police found traces of magnetism in the clearing where the UFO had been. And all six of the witnesses broke out in mild body rashes and felt numb afterward. Travis was interviewed under hypnosis to see if he was telling the truth about this incredible adventure. According to the hypnotist, Travis Walton was telling the truth.

Some of the leading UFO investigators believe this is a legitimate case. Others shake their heads and smile.

11

The Two Most Unique Encounters with Alien Beings

Of all the stories about encounters with alien beings, the case of Betty and Barney Hill is considered the most convincing by UFO researchers, and the case in Hopkinsville the weirdest.

The Case of Betty and Barney Hill

In September, 1961, Betty and Barney Hill, a middle-aged married couple, were driving in the White Mountains of New Hampshire, coming home from a weekend vacation in Canada. On a dark and lonely road late at night, they saw something peculiar — a glowing, brightly-lighted object, much brighter than the stars around it in the sky. It seemed to be keeping pace with their car, as if it were following them. It would move very fast, then it would change direction suddenly, swoop down, rise up, or stop and hover over one

JPI

This object, brighter than the moon, illustrates what Betty and Barney Hill first saw in New Hampshire in 1961. The photo was snapped in Missouri by a high school sophomore in 1973. He described it as "a radiant glow, very, very intense."

spot for a while. Betty Hill thought it might be a UFO but Barney argued with her that it had to be something "natural" — a star or a meteor.

As the object came down toward them, Barney stopped the car. He ran with his binoculars into a field for a better view. Betty stayed in the car. Barney could see that the object was round, much bigger than a jet airplane. Things that looked like wings, with red lights on their tips, appeared on the object. Then Barney was startled and terrified to see, through his binoculars, that inside the craft were odd-looking human-like creatures wearing black uniforms and staring down at him.

The UFO was near to the ground by then. Barney jumped back into the car and sped away down the road. They thought they had escaped; but after a few minutes, they heard buzzing sounds and beeping noises from above them and from inside the car itself. They began to feel sleepy and numb....Two hours later, about one o'clock in the morning, they were 35 miles down the highway. They had no idea where the time had gone or how they had traveled 35 miles. They decided not to tell anybody about this happening.

After a few days Betty and Barney began having nightmares every night and becoming more and more upset. They realized that the bad dreams had something to do with the UFO and those lost two hours, so they went to see a psychiatrist — Dr. Benjamin Simon.

Dr. Simon was an expert hypnotist who worked with people who had lost portions of their memory. Betty and Barney knew that the mind records and stores everything that happens to a person, even if the person can't remember it.

They hoped that Dr. Simon could help them to recapture the lost two hours.

Dr. Simon examined Betty and Barney separately many times, hypnotizing both of them. This amazing story is what came from each of them:

The object had landed on the road in front of them, blocking them from driving on. Several human-like beings got out of it and walked toward them, taking them aboard the vehicle.

The beings seemed mostly interested in performing a medical examination of the Hills, but they did not hurt them in any way. Barney had false teeth, which they removed from his mouth and looked at with great fascination. Then they tried to take out Betty's teeth, but hers were real and would not come out, which seemed to totally baffle the creatures.

Under hypnosis, both Barney and Betty reported that their captors assured them they would not be harmed.

Betty described the creatures as about five feet tall, with long noses, large eyes, and mouths that did not move. Their lips were bluish-gray. Their hair was dark.

Barney's description of the creatures was different in some ways. He did not see any hair on his captors; and he thought they did not have noses, just two slits for nostrils.

Both Betty and Barney agreed that the creatures talked to each other in a strange language. They used "words" and sounds that the Hills could not understand. Yet, when the beings talked with the Hills, they spoke in English.

Barney said, in the tapes that were made while he was under hypnosis: "I did not hear an actual voice. But in my mind, I knew what he was saying."[1]

Betty remembered that she asked one of the creatures if she could take something with her from the craft, as proof that this wild thing had really happened. The creature seemed generous and offered her anything she wished. Betty chose a book from the shelf that had Oriental-type printing on it. She also asked where their home was and was shown a map of various stars, with lines drawn between the stars. The creature told her that the heavy lines were trade routes; the thinner lines were to places they had visited from time to time. She asked again where his actual home was and he said she wouldn't understand even if he told her.

[1] Jacques Vallee, *Passport to Magonia* (Chicago: Henry Regnery Co., 1969).

After some time aboard the UFO, Betty and Barney were taken back to their car; but Betty was not allowed, after all, to take the book she had chosen. The creatures told the couple they would remember nothing of this incident. And, of course, they didn't, until placed under hypnosis.

Betty and Barney's meetings with the doctor who hypnotized them were put on tape. At one point Barney is telling the story of first seeing the UFO. "I'm out of the car, and I'm going down the road into the woods. There's an orange glow;

This sketch of the humanoids aboard the UFO which the Hills visited was drawn from the Hills' descriptions by APRO artist Norm Duke. The leader is poring over long charts.

APRO

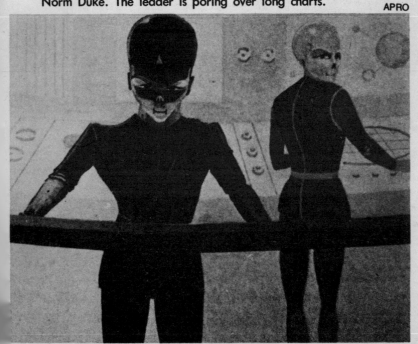

there's something there. Oh, oh, if only I had my gun; if only I had my gun. We go up the ramp....My feet just bumped, and I'm in a corridor. I don't want to go. I don't know where Betty is. I'm not harmed....I'm numb. I have no feeling in my fingers. My legs are numb. I'm on the table!"[2]

Betty reports what it was like when they were taken aboard the craft by one of the beings. "All I could say was, 'Barney, Barney, wake up.' [The being] asked me if his name was Barney. I didn't answer him 'cause I didn't think it was any of his business. And then when we got—I saw this—I knew they were gonna want us to go on it. I didn't want to go. I kept telling them I'm not gonna go—I don't want to go. And he said for me to go ahead, go, that they just wanted to do some simple tests. As soon as they were over with, I'd go back to the car."[3]

Of all the stories of capture by a UFO that have come down through the years, the Betty and Barney Hill case is considered, by scientists and investigators, one of the most convincing... strange as it is.

Do you believe it really happened to them?

[2]J. Allen Hynek, The UFO Experience: A Scientific Inquiry (New York: Ballantine, 1972) p. 181.

[3]Ibid. p. 183.

The Case in Hopkinsville

One of the weirdest of all UFO stories took place in Hopkinsville, Kentucky, in the summer of 1955. Many people think it's ridiculous. Many others take it seriously. A lot of research and investigation has been done on this case. It is a tale in which 11 people in the same family — seven adults and four children—all claim to have had the same incredible experience at the same time, to have seen the same amazing creatures.

Here is what they say happened: The entire family of Lucky Sutton was gathered in the Sutton farmhouse one night. One of the men had been outside walking near the property when he saw a UFO land in a gully near the farmhouse. He ran home to report this remarkable event, but everybody laughed at him, said he was crazy, and went about their business.

An hour later, after they had all but forgotten the silly story, their dog began barking ferociously in the backyard. Two of the men went to the back door to see what was all this commotion outside. There they witnessed the strangest sight of their lives: A small "man" who appeared to be glowing, walking slowly toward them, his arms raised over his head as if he were a prisoner. They described him as having very large eyes and oversized hands that looked like claws. He seemed completely friendly, even playful. But the Suttons were frightened, so the men grabbed their guns—one a .22 caliber rifle and the other a shotgun. When the creature was about 20 feet from the house, they shot.

But the creature, when struck by the bullets, simply glowed more, did a back-flip, bounced up on his feet, and dashed away. The sound of the bullets hitting him was described by one of the men, "just like I'd shot into a bucket."

A few minutes after that, another creature who looked exactly like the first appeared with his face pressed against the window of the farmhouse. The men fired shots again, this time through the window screen, which still bears the holes. Then they went outside to see if they'd hit the intruder, but when the first man stopped under the edge of the porch to look around, a hand reached down from the roof and playfully grabbed his hair!

Another little fellow appeared in a tree in the yard; they shot him too, and he too glowed even more, floated easily down to the ground, and scampered away. It should have been obvious to the Sutton family that these "elves" were harmless, merry, and antic. But the family was frightened. More creatures appeared in trees, on the roof. The family decided to stay in one room of the farmhouse, bolting all the doors and windows. During the next few hours, the visitors pressed their faces against the glass and walked around on the roof, but the Suttons stopped shooting at them.

After a few hours, the sounds quieted down and the family decided to make a run for it. At about 11:00 they ran outside, jumped into two cars, and sped to the nearest police station, seven miles away.

The police were skeptical of course; they had

never heard such a tale. But they returned to the area with the family to make a search. They could find nothing. They left.

Within a few moments after the police left, the glowing creatures reappeared, still doing their same shenanigans. The Suttons were so tired and drained that they all just went to sleep, despite the fact that the little men still surrounded their house and walked on the roof. By morning, these strange beings were gone.

A man in the area named Bud Ledwith was an announcer and engineer on a local radio station in Hopkinsville. The morning after this occurrence he interviewed the family on his radio show. He became very interested, personally, in the case. He performed a complete investigation, and he himself thoroughly believed their story. He could find no evidence of a hoax — these people were not seeking publicity and, in fact, suffered considerably from all the curiosity-seekers and sensation-seekers that surrounded them afterward.

At first, some of the experts thought perhaps there was a traveling circus in the area and some of the monkeys had escaped — monkeys which the Sutton family in the dark could have mistaken for alien creatures. But there were no circuses in the neighborhood, no evidence of monkeys, and besides — monkeys, when shot, fall. They don't float away.

Ledwith interviewed the seven adult Suttons in three different groups. He asked for detailed descriptions of the creatures. The descriptions matched...Ledwith made sketches from their descriptions.

The groups all agreed that the beings were between 2½ and 3½ feet tall, with bald heads that were egg-shaped. They made no sound and seemed weightless and they floated around in and out of the trees and the roof.

One of the most interesting parts of the Hopkinsville case is that the description of the humanoids is very much like descriptions given by people all over the world who have had close encounters with alien beings. The Suttons did not have television, radio, books, or newspapers, and it was highly unlikely that they were aware of other UFO stories. Yet their "little people" were exactly like those that have come down through recent history.

12

When Will We Know?

No one has ever captured a UFO or even chipped off a piece of it. And no one has ever brought an alien being home for dinner.

People who investigate UFO sightings dream of the day when they can get some "hard" evidence. Maybe a giant ship will break down in a field somewhere. The occupants will get out and march to the nearest garage for help.

Or maybe someday a craft will land in the middle of New York City. The occupants will stroll or float out of their vehicle and introduce themselves to the citizens. They will go on TV talk shows and tell about themselves. They will address the United Nations. Then, we will know. Then, we will be sure.

Until then, all we have are the reports of people

"... It started out with a glow above the horizon," said Ben Baron of Missouri about the sighting he snapped in 1973. (see also p. 67)

who claim to have seen or experienced UFOs and alien beings. Each one of us has to weigh the facts, judge the witnesses, and decide whether or not UFOs and their occupants really exist.

And even then, after we make up our own minds, we still won't know for sure.

More Books About UFOs and Their Occupants

Knight, David C., *Those Mysterious UFOs: The Story of Unidentified Flying Objects*. New York: Parents' Magazine Press, 1975. 64 pages, photographs, $5.95.

Strickland, Joshua, *Aliens On Earth!* New York: Grosset and Dunlap, Inc. 94 pages, illustrated with drawings, $4.95.

Paperbacks

Hynek, Dr. J. Allen, *The Hynek Report*. Paperback edition, New York: Dell Publishing Company, Inc., 1977. 304 pages, photographs, $1.95.

Hynek, Dr. J. Allen, *The UFO Experience: A Scientific Inquiry*. Paperback edition, New York: Ballantine Books, 1977. 309 pages, photographs, $2.25.